AI for Multi-State, International & Online Businesses

How AI Handles Complex Tax Jurisdictions

By Joe Correa

Published by Live Stronger Faster

This book is for educational and informational purposes only. The author and publisher are not engaged in rendering legal, financial, tax, or other professional advice. Readers should consult a qualified professional before making any financial decisions.

First Edition

Table of Contents

Introduction

The modern business no longer lives inside borders, offices, or even time zones, and for entrepreneurs running online platforms, digital agencies, SaaS companies, ecommerce stores, real estate investment groups, or global consulting firms, revenue now flows across state lines and national boundaries at the speed of the internet, but unfortunately tax rules still move at the speed of bureaucracy, and that mismatch has become one of the most expensive, dangerous, and confusing problems in the entire global economy, because a business can now sell to customers in California, Florida, Texas, New York, Canada, the European Union, and Asia on the same day while being legally registered in only one place, yet each of those transactions may create a tax obligation, reporting requirement, or compliance risk in a different jurisdiction, and without intelligent automation, most business owners are blind to what they actually owe, where they owe it, and how to stay compliant without overpaying, which is why artificial intelligence has become the single most powerful tool ever created for handling multi-state taxes, international tax law, VAT, GST, sales tax, nexus rules, transfer pricing, digital services taxes, and cross-border compliance. For decades, multinational corporations paid millions to armies of accountants, tax attorneys, and compliance officers to manage this complexity, but today even a solo entrepreneur running a Shopify store, an online course business, or a remote service company can trigger international tax exposure simply by selling a downloadable product, hiring a virtual assistant overseas, or advertising to foreign markets, and yet most small and mid-sized businesses still use accounting systems that were designed for a single state, a single currency, and a single tax authority, which leaves massive gaps that result in overpayment, underpayment, missed filings, penalties, audits, frozen bank accounts, and even criminal exposure in extreme cases, and the purpose of this book is to show you how AI now closes those gaps by continuously mapping your business activity across borders, tracking where value is created, where revenue is sourced, where customers are located, where employees or contractors are working, and where legal obligations are triggered, all in real time and without human error.

Artificial intelligence does not merely automate data entry, it understands patterns, jurisdictions, thresholds, treaties, and risk profiles, which means it can determine whether a digital sale to a customer in Germany requires VAT registration, whether a SaaS subscription sold to a California resident triggers sales tax nexus, whether a consulting contract in the UK creates permanent establishment risk, or whether a foreign contractor triggers payroll withholding obligations, and it can do this faster, more accurately, and more cheaply than any human tax team ever could, allowing businesses to operate globally without fear, because compliance is no longer a guessing game, it becomes a mathematically precise system of rules executed by software that never forgets, never sleeps, and never misses a deadline.

In the pre-AI world, international tax planning was reactive, meaning businesses discovered their exposure only after something went wrong, but AI turns tax into a proactive, predictive system that flags risks before they become liabilities, models tax outcomes before transactions occur, and automatically routes income, expenses, and profits through the most compliant and efficient structures available under the law, which means that instead of fearing multi-state and international growth, businesses can finally embrace it, because every sale, every invoice, every contractor payment, every ad dollar, and every royalty stream is continuously analyzed to ensure it is being taxed correctly, legally, and optimally in every jurisdiction that touches your business.

For online businesses, this is especially powerful because digital revenue does not behave like physical goods, and governments around the world have created overlapping and often conflicting rules to capture tax from software, subscriptions, digital downloads, online services, streaming platforms, affiliate income, influencer revenue, advertising, and remote consulting, and AI is now the only system capable of interpreting these rules at scale, applying them transaction by transaction, and generating the correct tax filings for each authority, whether that is a U.S. state revenue department, the IRS, the CRA in Canada, HMRC in the UK, or VAT agencies across the European Union, all while keeping your financial records synchronized and audit-ready.

Multi-state compliance inside the United States alone has become a nightmare for businesses, because economic nexus laws now require companies to collect and remit sales tax based on revenue and transaction volume rather than physical presence, which means an online business may have filing obligations in dozens of states without ever opening an office, and AI now solves this by continuously monitoring sales volume by state, identifying when thresholds are crossed, automatically registering the business, applying the correct tax rates, filing returns, and remitting payments on time, eliminating the risk of retroactive tax bills that can destroy cash flow and force businesses into insolvency.

International compliance adds another layer of complexity, because currency conversions, tax treaties, withholding taxes, digital service taxes, value-added taxes, and transfer pricing rules must all be accounted for, and AI excels at this because it can ingest treaty databases, live exchange rates, and jurisdiction-specific tax codes, then apply them to every transaction to determine what portion of revenue is taxable where, what credits are available, what exemptions apply, and how to legally minimize double taxation, which historically required teams of specialists but is now executed automatically by software running behind the scenes of your accounting and payment systems.

This book will show you how AI-driven tax platforms connect to your ecommerce stores, payment processors, payroll systems, banking platforms, crypto wallets, and international invoicing tools to create a unified, global tax brain for your company, one that sees every dollar the moment it is earned, categorizes it correctly, applies the correct jurisdictional rules, and prepares all required filings without human intervention, allowing founders, CFOs, and finance teams to focus on growth instead of compliance chaos.

You will also learn how AI helps businesses structure their international operations, deciding where to place entities, intellectual property, payment flows, and profit centers in a way that is fully compliant but also maximizes tax efficiency, using algorithmic simulations that compare thousands of legal structures across multiple countries to find the optimal configuration for your specific business model, something no traditional accountant could ever do manually, which means AI is no longer just a compliance tool, it is a strategic weapon for global profit optimization.

As governments continue to tighten reporting rules, introduce digital tax enforcement, and demand real-time data from businesses, the companies that thrive will be those that integrate AI into their tax and compliance systems, because manual processes cannot survive in a world where every transaction is tracked, every payment is reported, and every discrepancy is flagged by machine-learning systems on the government side, and this book gives you the blueprint to stay ahead of that curve by using AI to create a transparent, defensible, and optimized global tax infrastructure for your company.

By the end of this introduction and the chapters that follow, you will understand how artificial intelligence turns the chaos of multi-state and international taxation into a structured, automated, and profit-maximizing system that allows your business to operate anywhere in the world with confidence, clarity, and legal certainty, making borders irrelevant, compliance automatic, and growth unlimited, which is the true promise of AI-powered business taxation in the digital economy.

Chapter 1

How AI Maps Your Global Tax Footprint

Every business, whether it sells physical products, digital services, SaaS subscriptions, consulting hours, or online education, leaves behind a tax footprint that spreads across every jurisdiction where value is created, customers are served, payments are processed, or employees and contractors operate, and the first challenge of multi-state and international compliance has always been that most business owners do not even know where their footprint exists, which is why AI has become the foundation of modern tax management, because it can ingest massive volumes of transaction data from payment processors, ecommerce platforms, banks, payroll systems, ad networks, crypto wallets, and invoicing tools, then reconstruct a real-time map of where money is earned, where it flows, and which tax authorities have a legal claim to it, eliminating the dangerous blind spots that historically caused companies to unknowingly violate state and international tax laws.

AI performs this mapping by tracking four core dimensions simultaneously: the location of the customer, the location of the business entity, the location of the service or product delivery, and the location of labor or intellectual property, and when these dimensions cross borders, tax obligations are triggered, which means that a Shopify store based in Florida selling digital courses to customers in California, Canada, and Germany is not simply running one business, it is operating inside dozens of tax systems at once, and AI continuously monitors thresholds, treaty rules, and reporting requirements to determine when registration, collection, and filing obligations arise, something that is impossible to do accurately using spreadsheets or human memory.

In the United States alone, economic nexus laws have created a situation where sales volume, not physical presence, determines tax liability, meaning that a company can owe sales tax in a state it has never visited, and AI systems automatically track revenue and transaction counts by state, compare them to legal thresholds, and trigger compliance workflows when those thresholds are crossed, which prevents businesses from being hit with retroactive tax bills that can accumulate for years and wipe out profits overnight.

On the international side, AI must also account for VAT, GST, withholding taxes, digital services taxes, and permanent establishment risk, all of which depend on where customers are located, where servers are hosted, where employees work, and how contracts are structured, and modern AI platforms pull this data directly from IP addresses, billing addresses, payroll records, cloud providers, and legal documents, then apply treaty databases and jurisdiction-specific rules to determine what portion of revenue is taxable in each country and what reporting is required, giving businesses a constantly updated global compliance map that evolves as the company grows.

One of the most powerful capabilities of AI is its ability to detect hidden nexus, which occurs when businesses unknowingly create tax obligations through affiliate relationships, drop-shipping, fulfillment centers, digital marketplaces, influencer partnerships, or remote employees, and AI identifies these connections by analyzing transaction flows, shipping data, contract metadata, and platform integrations, ensuring that every place where value is created is properly accounted for before regulators discover it first.

AI also enables businesses to simulate future expansion before it happens, allowing them to see how entering a new market, hiring in another country, or launching a new product will affect their tax footprint, and these predictive models let companies choose the most tax-efficient growth paths rather than discovering expensive mistakes after the fact, which is why AI is not only a compliance engine but a strategic planning tool that guides global business expansion.

By the end of this chapter, it becomes clear that the first step in mastering multi-state and international taxation is visibility, and AI delivers that visibility by turning raw financial data into a living map of global tax exposure, giving businesses the power to operate anywhere in the world without fear, uncertainty, or regulatory surprise.

"The Day the Map Went Live"

When Daniel launched his online software company from a spare bedroom in Florida, he believed he was running a simple business, one product, one bank account, one tax return, and one set of rules, but within twelve months his SaaS platform had customers in forty-two states and twenty-three countries, yet his accounting software still treated everything as if it happened inside a single ZIP code, which is why the first letter from a foreign tax authority felt like a punch to the chest, because it claimed he owed VAT on sales he did not even realize were taxable, and that was only the beginning.

As Daniel dug deeper, he discovered that California considered his marketing affiliate a form of nexus, that New York claimed his digital subscriptions were subject to sales tax, that Canada wanted GST on his recurring billing, and that the European Union required VAT filings in multiple countries, and suddenly his profitable business felt like a legal minefield, until an AI-powered tax platform showed him something no human accountant ever had, a live, interactive map of his global tax footprint.

On the screen, Daniel watched as each sale lit up a different region, each contractor activated a new jurisdiction, and each ad campaign created a trail of potential obligations, and for the first time he could see exactly where his business existed in the eyes of governments around the world, not as one company, but as a network of tax relationships, and instead of fear, he felt clarity, because problems that are visible can be solved.

The AI flagged that he was approaching economic nexus in three U.S. states and warned him months before he would have crossed the threshold, giving him time to register and collect the correct taxes instead of being punished retroactively, and it also showed him that some of his European sales were eligible for special VAT treatment under digital service rules, saving him thousands of dollars he would have overpaid without the system.

As Daniel expanded into Asia and hired developers overseas, the AI automatically updated his compliance map, adjusting withholding calculations and treaty benefits in real time, and what once would have required an international tax firm now happened instantly, quietly, and accurately, behind the scenes of his business.

One year later, Daniel's company was ten times larger, operating in more than sixty countries, yet his tax compliance was simpler than it had ever been, because the AI had turned chaos into structure, borders into data points, and risk into something measurable and manageable.

Looking at the glowing world map on his dashboard, Daniel realized that he was no longer running a fragile startup trying to survive global complexity, he was running a truly international company powered by intelligence that never forgot, never miscalculated, and never left him exposed, and for the first time, he knew that growth no longer meant danger, it meant opportunity.

Chapter 2

Automating Sales Tax, VAT & Digital Services Taxes Across Borders

As businesses expand beyond a single state or country, the most immediate and financially dangerous form of tax exposure they face is transactional taxation, including U.S. sales tax, international value-added tax (VAT), goods and services tax (GST), and digital services taxes, because these taxes are charged on every sale, collected from customers, and remitted to governments, which means mistakes compound rapidly, turning small errors into massive liabilities, and AI has now become the only viable way to manage this complexity at scale, because it can calculate, apply, collect, report, and remit the correct tax for every transaction in every jurisdiction in real time without human intervention.

In the United States, economic nexus rules require businesses to register and collect sales tax once they exceed revenue or transaction thresholds in a state, but those thresholds vary by state and change frequently, and AI platforms continuously track sales activity across all states, compare that data against legal limits, and automatically trigger compliance workflows the moment a threshold is crossed, ensuring businesses never fall into the trap of unknowingly collecting tax too late or failing to register before they become legally obligated.

Internationally, VAT and GST systems operate very differently from U.S. sales tax, because taxes are charged at each stage of the supply chain and must be documented with precise invoice data, customer location verification, and reporting formats, and AI systems are uniquely suited for this because they validate billing addresses, IP locations, currency data, and customer classifications in real time, ensuring that each transaction is taxed correctly and that every digital receipt meets the legal standards of the country receiving the tax.

Digital services taxes add yet another layer of complexity, because many governments now tax revenue generated from online advertising, streaming, SaaS, and digital platforms regardless of where the company is based, and AI models analyze where users are located, where data is consumed, and where value is created to determine whether these taxes apply, then automatically allocate revenue and generate the required filings so businesses remain compliant without manually tracking millions of user interactions.

One of the greatest advantages of AI-driven tax automation is its ability to prevent overcollection, which is just as damaging as undercollection, because charging the wrong tax to customers can result in lawsuits, refund obligations, and regulatory scrutiny, and AI ensures that tax rates, exemptions, product classifications, and location-based rules are applied accurately, creating a system where every customer pays exactly what the law requires, no more and no less.

AI also handles multi-currency conversions, cross-border payment processor fees, and exchange rate fluctuations, ensuring that taxes are calculated on the correct taxable base in local currency and reported accurately to each tax authority, eliminating discrepancies that could trigger audits or penalties, even when thousands of transactions occur across dozens of countries every day.

By automating sales tax, VAT, GST, and digital services taxes through AI, businesses transform one of the most dangerous financial risks in global commerce into a predictable, automated, and fully auditable system, allowing them to scale revenue internationally without increasing compliance stress or financial uncertainty.

"The Invoice That Crossed the World"

When Sofia launched her online design platform, she imagined creativity flowing freely across borders, but she did not imagine tax invoices chasing her through every country her customers lived in, and the first time a European client asked why VAT was missing from their bill, she realized that global commerce was not just about selling, it was about complying with dozens of invisible rules that changed from one screen to the next.

At first, Sofia tried to manage everything manually, creating spreadsheets, checking country tax rates, and hoping she did not miss anything, but as her customer base exploded across North America, Europe, and Asia, the errors began to pile up, invoices were wrong, payments were delayed, and government notices started arriving in different languages, each demanding its share of her growing success.

Then she turned on an AI tax engine that connected directly to her payment system, and overnight her business changed, because every invoice now automatically calculated the correct sales tax, VAT, or digital services tax based on where her customer was located, how they paid, and what they purchased, and Sofia watched in amazement as what once took hours of manual work now happened in milliseconds.

A customer in France received a perfectly formatted VAT invoice, a client in Texas was charged the correct local sales tax, and a subscriber in Canada saw GST applied automatically, and no matter where the money came from, the AI knew exactly how to treat it, creating a seamless experience for both customers and governments. As her revenue climbed,

Sofia no longer worried about tax thresholds or regulatory changes, because the AI updated itself in real time, adjusting rates and rules as laws evolved, keeping her business compliant even as the world shifted beneath her feet.

One day she realized something extraordinary, her company was now selling in more than fifty countries, yet her tax compliance was stronger than it had ever been, because every transaction carried its own intelligence, guiding it safely through the maze of global regulations.

Looking at her dashboard, filled with neatly organized reports and perfectly balanced accounts, Sofia understood that global business was no longer about fighting complexity, it was about letting AI handle it, turning every invoice into a passport that allowed her company to travel the world without fear.

Chapter 3

AI-Driven Transfer Pricing, Profit Allocation & Cross-Border Optimization

When a business operates in more than one state or country, the most important and least understood question in global taxation is not how much revenue the company earns, but where that revenue is considered to have been earned, because every jurisdiction wants to tax the portion of profit that is attributed to its territory, its workers, its customers, or its intellectual property, and this process, known as transfer pricing and profit allocation, has historically been one of the most complex, expensive, and risky areas of international tax law, but artificial intelligence has now transformed it into a measurable, auditable, and optimizable system that allows businesses to legally align their global operations with the most efficient tax outcomes.

At its core, transfer pricing is the system that governs how money moves between related entities, such as a U.S. parent company paying a foreign subsidiary for software development, marketing, customer support, or intellectual property licensing, and if these internal transactions are not priced correctly according to arm's-length rules, governments can reclassify profits, impose penalties, or accuse the business of tax avoidance, which is why AI now plays a critical role in analyzing comparable market data, labor costs, intellectual property values, and transaction histories to determine fair, defensible pricing structures that comply with international standards while still optimizing profit placement.

AI systems ingest massive databases of real-world contracts, royalty agreements, service fees, and intercompany pricing benchmarks, then compare them against your company's internal transactions to calculate whether your transfer prices fall within acceptable ranges, flagging risks before they become liabilities and automatically generating documentation that proves your pricing is fair, which is something that previously required teams of lawyers and economists but can now be done continuously by software.

Profit allocation becomes even more important for digital and online businesses, where intellectual property, software, algorithms, customer data, and brand equity create most of the value, and AI models analyze where that value is actually created, whether in a development team in one country, a marketing operation in another, or a server infrastructure hosted elsewhere, then allocate profit accordingly in a way that satisfies tax authorities while still allowing the business to strategically place high-margin income in favorable jurisdictions.

One of the most powerful features of AI-driven tax platforms is their ability to simulate alternative corporate structures, allowing companies to see how profits, taxes, and compliance obligations would change if they moved intellectual property, created new subsidiaries, restructured service agreements, or altered their global payment flows, and these simulations give businesses a level of strategic foresight that was previously reserved for multinational corporations with billion-dollar budgets.

AI also ensures that transfer pricing compliance is not a once-a-year event but a continuous process, because it updates benchmarks, monitors transaction volumes, and adjusts pricing models as the business grows, preventing situations where outdated assumptions lead to sudden audit exposure, which is one of the most common causes of international tax disputes.

By turning transfer pricing and profit allocation into data-driven, algorithmic systems, AI allows businesses to operate globally with confidence, knowing that their internal transactions are fair, defensible, and optimized for both compliance and profitability, transforming what was once one of the greatest risks in international business into one of its greatest strategic advantages.

"Where the Profits Belonged"

When Marco built his digital marketing empire, he never thought about where the profits actually lived, he only cared that they kept growing, but as his company expanded into Europe, Latin America, and Southeast Asia, he found himself trapped in a web of conflicting tax claims, with each country insisting that it deserved a larger share of his success.

His developers in Argentina built the software, his ad teams in the Philippines ran the campaigns, his brand was registered in the United States, and his customers were everywhere, and suddenly governments wanted to know which part of that machine deserved to be taxed, and Marco realized that without a clear system, he could lose everything to audits and penalties.

That was when he deployed an AI-driven transfer pricing engine that analyzed every contract, every service agreement, and every line of revenue, mapping how value flowed through his company, and for the first time, Marco could see where profits were actually being created and where they legally belonged.

The AI adjusted internal pricing, documented the logic, and produced reports that satisfied regulators while also ensuring that high-margin income was placed where it could grow the fastest, and instead of fighting tax authorities, Marco now had proof on his side.

As his business continued to scale, the AI kept refining its models, adapting to new markets and new teams, making sure his structure remained compliant even as it became more complex.

Years later, when Marco faced his first international audit, it lasted less than a week, because every number, every payment, and every profit allocation was already supported by data and documentation generated by the system.

Looking at the final clearance letter, Marco realized that intelligence, not fear, now governed his global business, and by letting AI decide where profits belonged, he had secured both his growth and his peace of mind.

Chapter 4

Managing Remote Workers, Contractors & Permanent Establishment Risk With AI

As businesses scale beyond borders, the most underestimated and fastest-triggering source of tax exposure is not revenue, sales tax, or even profit allocation, but people, because the moment a business hires an employee, engages a contractor, or relies on outsourced labor in another state or country, it may create payroll obligations, withholding requirements, social security contributions, employment law exposure, and in some cases permanent establishment risk, which can subject the entire company to foreign corporate taxation, and artificial intelligence has now become the only reliable way to monitor, manage, and neutralize these risks in real time.

Permanent establishment risk occurs when a business is deemed to have a sufficient physical or economic presence in a jurisdiction to justify corporate taxation there, and this can be triggered by something as simple as a remote employee negotiating contracts, managing customers, developing core intellectual property, or representing the company locally, which means many modern online businesses unintentionally expose themselves to foreign corporate tax simply by embracing remote work, and AI systems are uniquely equipped to detect these risks by analyzing job roles, contract language, communication patterns, revenue attribution, and geographic activity simultaneously.

AI platforms connect directly to payroll systems, HR platforms, contractor management tools, and collaboration software to track where work is actually being performed, not just where workers claim to live, and this distinction matters because tax authorities increasingly look beyond formal addresses and examine digital footprints, login activity, IP data, meeting records, and decision-making authority, and AI can synthesize these signals into a clear assessment of whether a worker's activities cross the line from support functions into revenue-generating or decision-making roles that create taxable presence.

For multi-state U.S. businesses, AI automates payroll tax withholding, unemployment insurance, workers' compensation classification, and state-specific employment filings by continuously adjusting based on employee location changes, role shifts, and compensation updates, eliminating the administrative nightmare that traditionally followed remote hiring, while also preventing penalties caused by late or incorrect filings across multiple jurisdictions.

Internationally, AI becomes even more powerful by evaluating tax treaties, labor laws, and permanent establishment thresholds country by country, determining whether a contractor should legally be classified as an employee, whether payroll taxes are required, whether social contributions must be paid, and whether the company must register locally, and these determinations are updated dynamically as worker responsibilities evolve, preventing situations where a contractor slowly becomes a hidden tax liability without the company realizing it.

AI also enables businesses to restructure remote work intelligently, recommending safer role definitions, contract terms, reporting lines, and operational boundaries that reduce permanent establishment exposure while still allowing global teams to function effectively, and this proactive design approach transforms compliance from a reactive defense into a strategic architecture that supports growth without triggering unnecessary tax burdens.

By automating workforce compliance and continuously monitoring cross-border labor activity, AI allows businesses to operate globally without fear that a single hire or contractor could unknowingly expose the entire company to foreign taxation, audits, or penalties, making remote work sustainable, scalable, and legally defensible in a world where borders are digital but tax enforcement is increasingly sophisticated.

"The Employee Who Changed Everything"

Ethan believed remote work was freedom, not risk, because when he launched his online analytics company, he hired talent wherever he found it, developers in Eastern Europe, marketers in South America, support teams in Asia, and consultants scattered across time zones, all connected by Slack, Zoom, and shared dashboards, and for years the system worked beautifully, revenue grew, customers were happy, and the company felt untethered from geography, until one unexpected email shattered that illusion.

The message came from a tax authority Ethan had never dealt with before, written in formal language and referencing corporate income tax, payroll obligations, and something called permanent establishment, and at first he assumed it was a mistake, because his company had no offices, no subsidiaries, and no physical presence in that country, but as he read further, his stomach tightened, because the letter named one of his contractors, a senior account manager who had been negotiating client renewals and managing local partnerships, and suddenly Ethan realized that one person, doing their job too well, had changed the legal reality of his business. He spent weeks scrambling, calling accountants, lawyers, and advisors, each giving conflicting opinions, some saying it was nothing, others warning it could expose years of back taxes, penalties, and interest, and the deeper he dug, the more he understood how fragile his global structure really was, because no one had ever mapped what his people were actually doing, only where he thought they were working.

That was when he implemented an AI workforce compliance system, not as a luxury, but as a last line of defense, and within hours of connecting payroll, contracts, and collaboration tools, the system illuminated patterns he had never seen, which employees were signing contracts, which contractors had authority over pricing, which team members influenced customer decisions, and how those activities aligned with tax rules across dozens of jurisdictions.

The AI flagged multiple hidden risks, not just the one country that had already contacted him, but others he had unknowingly approached, and it didn't just warn him, it offered solutions, role adjustments, contract updates, reporting changes, and structural safeguards that reduced exposure without dismantling his global team, turning panic into a plan.

Over the next several months, Ethan restructured responsibilities, updated agreements, and shifted decision-making authority to safer jurisdictions, guided entirely by simulations run by the AI, and when the tax authority followed up, he responded not with uncertainty, but with documentation, timelines, and evidence showing that the company had acted responsibly and compliantly, which transformed an adversarial inquiry into a cooperative resolution.

As his business continued to grow, the AI monitored every new hire and contractor automatically, recalculating risk as roles evolved, alerting him before thresholds were crossed rather than after damage was done, and what once felt like walking on a legal tightrope now felt like standing on solid ground.

Years later, when Ethan spoke to other founders about scaling globally, he no longer talked about tools or platforms first, he talked about awareness, because he learned that global businesses are not defined by where their offices are, but by where decisions are made, where value is created, and where people act on behalf of the company, and without intelligence watching those movements, growth is not freedom, it is exposure.

Looking back, Ethan realized that the employee who once terrified him had actually saved his company, because that moment forced him to build a system that understood his business better than he ever had, one that transformed remote work from a hidden liability into a controlled, compliant, and powerful engine for global expansion, proving that in the age of AI, the safest way to grow everywhere is to understand everything.

Chapter 5

AI, Tax Treaties, Withholding Rules & Double Taxation Elimination

As businesses expand internationally, one of the most misunderstood and financially destructive risks they face is double taxation, which occurs when two or more jurisdictions claim the right to tax the same income, and without careful planning, businesses can find themselves paying tax on the same dollar multiple times, once where the income is earned, again where it is received, and sometimes again where the business is headquartered, and historically, avoiding this outcome required deep expertise in international tax treaties, withholding rules, foreign tax credits, and cross-border reporting systems, but artificial intelligence has now become the most effective tool ever created for navigating this complexity automatically and continuously.

Tax treaties exist to prevent double taxation by defining how income is classified, which country has primary taxing rights, and how credits or exemptions should be applied, but these treaties are dense, technical documents filled with exceptions, thresholds, and conditional language that even experienced professionals struggle to interpret consistently, and AI systems now ingest treaty databases from around the world, compare them against a company's specific income streams, and determine in real time which treaty provisions apply to each transaction, eliminating guesswork and reducing the risk of both overpayment and noncompliance.

Withholding taxes present another major challenge, because many countries require businesses to withhold tax at the source when making payments to foreign vendors, contractors, licensors, or subsidiaries, and failure to withhold correctly can result in penalties even if the recipient later pays tax, and AI platforms now automatically classify payments, identify applicable withholding rates, apply treaty reductions when available, and generate the necessary documentation to support reduced or zero withholding, ensuring that businesses comply with local laws while preserving cash flow.

AI also manages foreign tax credits by tracking taxes paid abroad, categorizing them correctly, and matching them against domestic tax obligations so that businesses receive full credit for taxes already paid, preventing double taxation while maintaining audit-ready documentation that supports every credit claimed, which is critical because improperly documented credits are often denied during audits even when they are legally valid. Currency fluctuations, timing differences, and mismatched reporting periods add further complexity to international taxation, and AI resolves these issues by standardizing data across currencies, reconciling timing differences, and aligning reporting schedules so that income and taxes are matched accurately across jurisdictions, eliminating discrepancies that could trigger audits or disputes.

One of the most powerful capabilities of AI is its ability to model treaty outcomes before transactions occur, allowing businesses to see how changing payment structures, contract terms, or entity locations would affect withholding, credits, and overall tax burden, and this predictive intelligence transforms international tax planning from a reactive process into a proactive strategy that minimizes tax friction while remaining fully compliant.

By automating treaty interpretation, withholding compliance, and foreign tax credit optimization, AI enables businesses to operate globally without fear of being taxed twice on the same income, turning international expansion from a financial risk into a structured, predictable, and optimized process that supports long-term growth and profitability.

"The Same Dollar, Twice Claimed"

When Lena's consulting firm crossed its first international border, she celebrated the new client, the new revenue, and the validation that her expertise mattered beyond her home country, but celebration turned to confusion months later when she noticed something unsettling in her financial reports, the same income appeared to be taxed twice, once overseas and once at home, and no one could clearly explain why.

At first, Lena assumed it was a bookkeeping error, but as more international clients came on board, the pattern repeated itself, foreign taxes withheld at the source, domestic taxes assessed on the full amount, and a growing sense that her success was being quietly eroded by invisible rules she did not fully understand, and the more advisors she consulted, the more fragmented the answers became, each one focusing on a single country, a single rule, or a single form, without seeing the whole picture.

The breaking point came when a large international contract required a significant withholding tax that immediately reduced her cash flow, even though she was told she might be able to claim a credit later, and the uncertainty terrified her, because running a growing business on promises of future refunds felt like building on sand, and she realized she needed a system that understood global taxation as a living network, not a stack of disconnected regulations.

That was when Lena integrated an AI-driven international tax engine into her operations, and the first thing it did was map every dollar she earned, showing where it originated, where tax was withheld, which treaty applied, and how credits could be claimed, and for the first time, Lena could see how the same dollar had been claimed by multiple governments, not because of wrongdoing, but because of incomplete coordination.

The AI began restructuring payment flows automatically, applying treaty reductions at the source, generating residency certificates, and aligning contracts with treaty definitions, and slowly, almost invisibly, the pressure eased, withholding rates dropped, credits were applied correctly, and Lena's cash flow stabilized, not because she had become an international tax expert, but because intelligence now handled complexity on her behalf.

As her firm expanded into new regions, the AI adapted continuously, pulling updated treaty provisions, recalculating obligations, and flagging risks before payments were made, and instead of fearing international contracts, Lena now reviewed simulations that showed exactly how each deal would be taxed before she signed it, turning uncertainty into informed choice.

Years later, when Lena looked back at the early days of international growth, she remembered the anxiety of watching income disappear into overlapping tax systems, and she realized that the true cost was not just money, but confidence, because uncertainty had made her hesitant to grow, and only when AI removed that uncertainty did her business truly become global.

Standing in her office, reviewing a dashboard that showed clean, reconciled global tax flows, Lena understood that the problem had never been international business itself, but the lack of coordination between systems, and by letting AI become the translator between governments, treaties, and transactions, she had reclaimed control over her income, her growth, and her future, proving that no business should ever have to pay twice for the same success.

Chapter 6

AI-Powered Global Reporting, Documentation & Audit Survival

As businesses operate across multiple states and countries, compliance does not end with calculating and paying the correct taxes, because the true battleground of global taxation is documentation, reporting, and audit defense, where even a technically correct tax position can collapse if it is not supported by the right records, the right formats, and the right timing, and this is where artificial intelligence has become indispensable, transforming reporting from a reactive administrative burden into a proactive, always-on compliance shield that protects businesses long before any audit notice arrives.

Governments around the world are rapidly shifting from periodic, manual audits to continuous, data-driven oversight, requiring businesses to submit increasingly detailed reports on transactions, payroll, cross-border payments, transfer pricing, VAT, sales tax, and digital services revenue, often in real time or near real time, and AI systems are uniquely suited to meet this demand because they collect, organize, reconcile, and validate data continuously rather than scrambling to assemble records after the fact. AI-driven reporting platforms automatically generate jurisdiction-specific filings, ensuring that each tax authority receives information in the exact format it requires, whether that is a U.S. state sales tax return, a VAT MOSS filing in the European Union, a transfer pricing master file, a country-by-country report, or a foreign payroll declaration, eliminating the risk of rejection, penalties, or audits triggered simply by formatting errors or missing data fields.

Documentation is the silent foundation of audit survival, and AI excels at maintaining it because it never forgets to save contracts, invoices, payment records, currency conversions, IP allocations, payroll logs, treaty certificates, and compliance decisions, linking each document directly to the transaction or rule it supports, creating a living audit trail that is far stronger than traditional file storage systems that rely on human discipline and memory.

When audits do occur, AI fundamentally changes the experience, because instead of reacting defensively, businesses can respond instantly with structured data, supporting evidence, and clear explanations generated directly from the system, demonstrating transparency, consistency, and compliance, which often shortens audits dramatically and reduces the likelihood of aggressive enforcement actions. AI also detects reporting inconsistencies before authorities do, identifying mismatches between jurisdictions, timing differences, or data discrepancies that could raise red flags, and resolving them proactively, preventing audits from being triggered in the first place, which is one of the most powerful yet least visible benefits of intelligent compliance systems.

By automating global reporting and audit readiness, AI allows businesses to operate internationally with confidence, knowing that every number, every filing, and every explanation is already prepared, defensible, and aligned across borders, turning compliance from a source of fear into a competitive advantage that supports sustainable, scalable growth.

"The Audit That Never Broke Them"

The letter arrived on a quiet Monday morning, slipped between routine emails and calendar reminders, and at first Maya barely noticed it, until she saw the words "Notice of Examination" printed in stark, official language, and in that moment, the air in her office seemed to change, because even though her global ecommerce business was thriving, she knew that an audit, especially a multi-country one, had the power to unravel years of progress if even a single thread was weak.

Maya had built her company slowly and deliberately, selling digital products and physical goods across continents, hiring remote teams, paying foreign vendors, and reinvesting profits into growth, and while she believed she had done everything correctly, she also knew how fragile compliance could be when stretched across borders, currencies, and constantly changing regulations, and the fear was not that she had done something wrong, but that she could not prove she had done everything right.

In the early days, Maya had watched other founders panic during audits, digging through emails, searching for missing invoices, reconstructing decisions made years earlier, and negotiating from a position of exhaustion and uncertainty, and she had promised herself she would never be in that position, which is why she had invested early in an AI-driven global reporting system, even when it felt excessive at the time.

When she opened the AI dashboard after reading the audit notice, she did not see chaos, she saw structure, timelines, transaction flows, jurisdictional summaries, and linked documentation, all aligned and reconciled, and instead of panic, she felt something unexpected, calm, because the system had already anticipated the questions auditors would ask and had prepared the answers long before the letter arrived.

The audit expanded quickly, crossing state lines and international borders, with multiple authorities requesting records, explanations, and reconciliations, but each request was met with precise, organized responses generated directly from the system, complete with supporting evidence and contextual explanations that showed not just what had happened, but why it complied with the law, and as weeks passed, the tone of the audit shifted from adversarial to procedural.

Auditors asked fewer follow-up questions, timelines shortened, and issues that could have escalated into disputes were resolved quietly through documentation that left little room for interpretation, and Maya realized that the AI had not just stored data, it had told a coherent story of her business, one that regulators could understand and verify without suspicion.

As the final reports were issued, each authority closed its examination with minimal adjustments and no penalties, and when the last notice arrived confirming the audit's conclusion, Maya sat back and reflected on what could have been a defining crisis, but instead became a confirmation that preparation, not reaction, determines outcomes in global business.

Months later, when new founders asked her about scaling internationally, Maya did not talk first about markets, platforms, or growth strategies, she talked about resilience, about building systems that assume scrutiny, that welcome transparency, and that transform compliance into confidence, because she learned that success is not measured by avoiding audits, but by surviving them without breaking.

Looking at her global operations now, Maya understood that intelligence was not just about maximizing profit or minimizing tax, it was about building a business strong enough to withstand attention, complexity, and growth simultaneously, and in a world where data never sleeps and regulators never forget, the audit that never broke them became the quiet proof that AI was not a tool, but the backbone of her company's future.

Chapter 7

Scaling Globally Without Breaking Compliance: How AI Enables Confident Expansion

Growth has always been the ultimate test of a business's tax and compliance systems, because what works at a small scale almost never survives success, and nowhere is this more evident than in multi-state and international expansion, where each new market adds layers of tax law, reporting obligations, employment rules, and regulatory scrutiny that compound exponentially, and artificial intelligence has now become the only realistic way for businesses to scale globally without collapsing under their own complexity.

The moment a business enters a new state or country, it does not merely add another revenue stream, it adds a new compliance universe, complete with unique filing calendars, thresholds, classifications, audit standards, and enforcement technologies, and without AI, most companies attempt to manage this growth manually, relying on fragmented advisors, spreadsheets, and reactive fixes, which inevitably leads to blind spots, delays, and costly mistakes that only surface once the business is large enough to attract regulatory attention. AI changes this dynamic by transforming expansion into a modeled, simulated, and monitored process rather than a leap of faith, because before a company enters a new jurisdiction, AI can project the tax consequences, compliance requirements, payroll obligations, sales tax exposure, permanent establishment risk, and reporting costs associated with that move, allowing leaders to make informed decisions about where and how to grow instead of discovering the price of expansion after it has already been paid.

As businesses scale, transaction volume increases dramatically, and with it the risk of small errors multiplying into major liabilities, but AI systems thrive under scale, continuously reconciling millions of data points across jurisdictions, identifying anomalies, and correcting inconsistencies before they become systemic problems, which means that growth actually strengthens compliance rather than weakening it when intelligence is embedded at the core of operations.

One of the most critical advantages of AI-driven scalability is consistency, because regulators do not just look for correctness in individual filings, they look for coherence across systems, years, and jurisdictions, and AI ensures that tax positions, classifications, and reporting logic remain aligned globally, even as the business evolves, preventing contradictions that could trigger audits or accusations of manipulation.

AI also enables decentralized growth without decentralized risk, allowing teams, subsidiaries, and partners around the world to operate autonomously while remaining connected to a centralized compliance intelligence layer that enforces rules, standards, and oversight uniformly, ensuring that local actions never jeopardize global integrity.

Ultimately, AI allows businesses to scale with confidence, knowing that every new market, customer, and employee is absorbed into a system that understands the implications instantly, adjusts automatically, and documents everything continuously, making global expansion not a gamble, but a controlled, strategic progression supported by intelligence rather than hope.

"Growth Was the Risk"

When Arjun launched his digital logistics platform, growth was the dream, not the danger, because every new customer validated his idea and every new market proved the business could scale, but as expansion accelerated, something subtle began to change, not in revenue or visibility, but in pressure, because behind every new country added to his dashboard was a silent increase in complexity that no one on his team fully understood. At first, the signs were easy to ignore, a delayed filing here, a confusing notice there, a payroll question that took weeks to answer, and Arjun told himself these were normal growing pains, the price of success, but the deeper the company expanded into new regions, the more those pains began to feel like fractures, because each market introduced rules that contradicted the last, and no single advisor could see the entire picture.

The real turning point came when a major investor asked a simple question during a board meeting, "Can you explain your global compliance structure?" and Arjun realized, with a cold clarity, that while he could explain his product, his growth metrics, and his vision, he could not confidently explain how his company remained compliant across all the places it now operated, and that gap threatened everything he had built.

Determined not to let complexity undo success, Arjun implemented an AI-driven global compliance system, not to fix a crisis, but to prevent one, and the first thing it did was reveal how fragile his growth had become, highlighting overlapping obligations, inconsistent classifications, and emerging risks that no human had stitched together before, and seeing it all at once was terrifying, but it was also empowering, because for the first time, the problem was defined.

The AI did not tell him to stop growing, it taught him how to grow intelligently, simulating expansion paths, ranking markets by risk-adjusted return, and showing how small structural changes could dramatically reduce compliance exposure, and instead of reacting to problems after they appeared, Arjun began choosing growth moves that aligned with long-term stability.

As the company continued to scale, the AI adapted continuously, absorbing new data, recalculating obligations, and enforcing consistency across regions, and growth no longer felt like a threat to control, but a process that strengthened the system with every additional data point, turning complexity into resilience.

Years later, when Arjun looked back at the moment he almost lost confidence in his own expansion, he realized that growth itself had never been the risk, ignorance had been, and by giving his business intelligence equal to its ambition, he had built something rare, a global company that could grow without fear of itself.

Standing in a conference room overlooking a skyline far from where the idea had begun, Arjun understood that success in a borderless world belongs not to the fastest movers, but to those who build systems strong enough to sustain motion, and by letting AI guide expansion instead of chasing it blindly, he had ensured that growth would never again be the most dangerous part of the journey.

Chapter 8

Future-Proofing Global Compliance: How AI Adapts to Constant Legal Change

The final and most underestimated challenge of operating a multi-state and international business is not understanding today's tax rules, but surviving tomorrow's, because tax law is not static, it is a living system that evolves constantly in response to political pressure, economic cycles, technological change, and government demand for revenue, and businesses that build compliance systems based only on current regulations are quietly building obsolescence into their operations, which is why artificial intelligence has become essential not merely for compliance, but for future-proofing compliance itself.

Across the world, governments are accelerating regulatory change, introducing real-time reporting, expanding digital services taxes, redefining nexus thresholds, tightening permanent establishment standards, and deploying their own AI systems to detect discrepancies faster and more aggressively than ever before, and this environment makes manual compliance fundamentally unsustainable, because humans cannot track, interpret, and implement thousands of regulatory updates across jurisdictions fast enough to remain consistently compliant at scale.

AI addresses this problem by treating tax and regulatory change as a data stream rather than a periodic event, continuously ingesting updates from legislation, court rulings, administrative guidance, treaty revisions, and enforcement patterns, then integrating those changes directly into compliance logic, calculations, and reporting workflows, ensuring that businesses remain aligned with the law as it evolves rather than reacting after the fact.

One of the most powerful aspects of AI-driven compliance is its ability to compare regulatory intent with actual enforcement behavior, identifying how authorities apply rules in practice rather than how they are written on paper, and this allows businesses to adjust proactively, aligning their operations not only with legal requirements but with enforcement reality, reducing audit risk and uncertainty even as laws shift.

AI also enables scenario planning at a level that was previously impossible, allowing businesses to model how proposed laws, treaty renegotiations, or policy shifts would affect their tax burden, compliance obligations, and operational structure, and this foresight transforms regulatory change from a disruptive force into a strategic input that guides decision-making long before changes take effect.

As businesses scale globally, the cost of regulatory surprise increases exponentially, but AI absorbs that risk by continuously monitoring exposure, recalculating obligations, and updating documentation automatically, ensuring that compliance systems evolve alongside the business and the law simultaneously rather than falling behind one or the other.

By embedding intelligence at the core of compliance, businesses move beyond survival mode and into resilience, creating global operations that can adapt to change without disruption, panic, or costly restructuring, proving that in a world of constant legal evolution, the only sustainable compliance strategy is one that evolves faster than the rules themselves.

"The Rules Changed Overnight"

The announcement came without warning, buried in a late-night regulatory bulletin that most businesses would not read until weeks later, but for companies operating across borders, the change was seismic, new reporting thresholds, new definitions of digital presence, and new penalties for noncompliance, all effective almost immediately, and for many founders, it marked the beginning of chaos. For Clara, the CEO of a rapidly growing online education platform, the news arrived quietly, flagged by an alert from the AI compliance system she had implemented years earlier, and while other companies slept through the announcement, her dashboard lit up with simulations, risk assessments, and updated compliance pathways before dawn, and she knew instantly that the world had shifted again.

In the early years of her company, Clara had tried to keep up with regulations manually, subscribing to newsletters, attending webinars, and relying on advisors who were always a step behind the latest changes, and she remembered the stress of discovering new obligations months too late, scrambling to fix problems that had already compounded into liabilities, and promising herself that if the business ever scaled, she would never allow compliance to remain reactive.

As the company expanded into dozens of countries, Clara invested in AI not to save time, but to gain awareness, and that investment now revealed its true value, because while competitors panicked, unsure how new laws would affect their revenue models, Clara's system recalculated everything automatically, identifying which markets were impacted, which customers fell under new definitions, and which reporting workflows needed to change immediately. The AI did not just adjust calculations, it explained the implications, showing how the new rules aligned with emerging enforcement trends, how regulators were likely to interpret gray areas, and how minor operational changes could reduce exposure without sacrificing growth, and instead of reacting emotionally, Clara made decisions calmly, guided by intelligence rather than fear.

In the weeks that followed, regulators intensified scrutiny, issuing notices and inquiries to businesses that had failed to adapt in time, and Clara watched as competitors faced penalties, delayed payments, and reputational damage, not because they had acted recklessly, but because they had been unaware, and awareness, she realized, was now the most valuable currency in global business.

Years later, when Clara reflected on that moment of overnight change, she understood that it was not the rule itself that defined success or failure, but the speed of adaptation, and by building a company whose compliance system learned and evolved continuously, she had ensured that no single regulatory shift could ever threaten its foundation.

Standing before a new generation of founders, Clara no longer framed compliance as a burden or a cost, but as an adaptive system, one that must be designed to learn faster than the environment changes, because in a world where laws evolve as quickly as technology, survival belongs to those who build intelligence into everything they do.

Chapter 9

From Compliance to Competitive Advantage: How AI Turns Global Tax Complexity Into Strategic Power

For most businesses, tax compliance has historically been treated as a defensive necessity, something to endure, minimize, or outsource in the hope that it never becomes a problem, but in a world where businesses operate across borders, currencies, platforms, and regulatory regimes, that mindset is no longer sufficient, because compliance is no longer just about avoiding penalties, it is about how intelligently a company navigates complexity, allocates resources, and positions itself for sustainable growth, and artificial intelligence is the catalyst that transforms compliance from a cost center into a strategic asset.

When AI is embedded into a company's global tax and compliance infrastructure, it does more than calculate obligations and generate filings, it reveals patterns that human analysis cannot see, identifying where margins are strongest after tax, which jurisdictions offer the best balance of opportunity and risk, how regulatory friction affects cash flow timing, and where structural inefficiencies quietly erode profitability, and this visibility allows leadership teams to make decisions based not just on revenue potential, but on true, after-tax performance across markets.

AI-driven compliance systems continuously analyze data across jurisdictions, comparing tax rates, incentives, credits, reporting costs, and enforcement intensity, creating a dynamic map of global opportunity that evolves as laws change and the business grows, and this map becomes a strategic tool, guiding expansion, pricing, investment, and hiring decisions with a level of precision that was previously impossible, especially for small and mid-sized companies without massive advisory budgets.

One of the most powerful shifts AI enables is the alignment of tax strategy with operational strategy, because instead of designing the business first and fixing tax problems later, companies can now design operations with tax intelligence embedded from the start, choosing entity structures, supply chains, workforce models, and revenue flows that are optimized for both compliance and profitability, reducing friction at every stage of growth.

AI also democratizes strategic tax planning by making advanced analysis accessible in real time, not just during annual planning cycles, allowing businesses to test scenarios continuously, evaluate the tax impact of new products, partnerships, or markets before committing resources, and adjust course quickly when conditions change, turning agility into a measurable competitive advantage.

As governments deploy their own AI systems to monitor compliance, businesses that rely on manual processes or fragmented advisors will increasingly fall behind, not necessarily because they are noncompliant, but because they lack the speed, consistency, and transparency that modern enforcement expects, while companies that operate with AI-driven compliance will find themselves better aligned with regulatory systems, experiencing fewer disputes, faster resolutions, and lower overall risk.

Ultimately, AI reframes global tax complexity not as an obstacle, but as a differentiator, because companies that master compliance intelligence can move faster, enter markets more confidently, allocate capital more efficiently, and build trust with regulators, partners, and investors, proving that in the modern global economy, the smartest companies do not merely survive complexity, they use it to win.

"The Advantage No One Saw"

When Noah founded his cross-border fintech platform, he knew the product had potential, but he also knew the space was crowded with competitors racing toward the same markets, offering similar features, similar pricing, and similar promises, and for a long time, he believed speed alone would determine who survived, because whoever expanded fastest would capture customers before regulation could catch up.

In the early days, Noah focused relentlessly on growth, onboarding users across continents, partnering with local providers, and pushing into new jurisdictions as soon as demand appeared, and while revenue climbed, so did complexity, with each new market introducing tax rules, reporting obligations, and compliance costs that no one fully understood, and advisors warned him to slow down, to consolidate, to wait until things stabilized, but slowing down felt like surrender.

The turning point came not from a crisis, but from a realization, during a strategic review where Noah noticed that two markets with similar revenue profiles produced very different net results after tax, compliance costs, and regulatory friction were accounted for, and he realized that growth alone was not the metric that mattered, intelligence was, and without understanding how complexity affected performance, his company was flying blind. That insight led Noah to integrate an AI-driven global compliance and tax intelligence system, not to fix a problem, but to understand his business more deeply, and almost immediately, the system began surfacing insights no human team had identified, showing which markets generated the highest after-tax margins, which regulatory environments slowed cash flow, and which expansion paths looked attractive on the surface but were quietly draining resources.

Armed with this information, Noah made decisions his competitors could not see coming, pulling back from markets that looked large but underperformed after compliance costs, doubling down on jurisdictions where incentives and efficient structures amplified profitability, and restructuring operations to reduce friction without sacrificing reach, and while others chased growth headlines, Noah optimized substance.

Over time, the difference became undeniable, because while competitors struggled with audits, cash flow delays, and regulatory surprises, Noah's company moved with confidence, entering new markets methodically, pricing products with full awareness of tax impact, and reinvesting profits strategically, and investors began to notice that this company did not just grow fast, it grew cleanly, predictably, and sustainably.

Years later, when Noah was asked what gave his company an edge in such a competitive industry, he did not talk about features or branding, he talked about visibility, about understanding how every decision played out across borders, systems, and regulators, and he explained that while others saw compliance as a brake on innovation, he saw it as a source of insight that guided innovation intelligently.

Standing on a stage at an international conference, Noah looked out at an audience of founders facing the same complexity he once feared, and he realized that the advantage his company had built was invisible to those who still treated compliance as a burden, because the true edge was not speed alone, but the ability to move with clarity in a world where complexity never stops growing, and by letting AI turn global tax intelligence into strategy, he had built something competitors could not easily replicate, a business that did not just operate globally, but understood the global system well enough to thrive within it.

Chapter 10

Building the Autonomous Global Tax Engine: Where AI Takes Full Control

The ultimate destination of AI-driven multi-state and international taxation is not partial automation, decision support, or efficiency gains layered on top of human judgment, but the creation of a fully autonomous global tax engine, a system capable of sensing business activity as it happens, interpreting legal obligations across jurisdictions, executing compliant actions in real time, and continuously learning from outcomes without requiring constant human intervention, and this shift represents the most profound transformation in the history of business compliance.

Traditional tax systems were designed for an era when transactions were slow, localized, and infrequent, when reporting cycles were annual or quarterly, and when human professionals could reasonably keep pace with regulatory change, but modern digital businesses operate continuously, across borders, currencies, platforms, and legal regimes, and this mismatch has created a structural failure where compliance systems lag behind reality, which AI resolves by operating at the same speed and scale as the business itself. An autonomous tax engine begins with total integration, connecting directly to payment processors, banks, ecommerce platforms, payroll systems, HR tools, contracts, advertising platforms, and operational software, creating a unified data environment where every transaction, decision, and movement of value is immediately visible, categorized, and assessed for tax relevance, eliminating delays, blind spots, and manual reconciliation entirely.

Once data is ingested, AI applies jurisdiction-specific logic automatically, determining taxability, classification, sourcing rules, treaty applicability, withholding requirements, and reporting obligations for each transaction in real time, and unlike static rule engines, modern AI systems continuously refine their interpretations based on regulatory updates, enforcement patterns, and historical outcomes, allowing the system to evolve alongside the law rather than constantly falling behind it.

Execution is the defining feature of autonomy, because the system does not stop at analysis, it registers entities, applies tax at the point of sale, withholds when required, remits payments, files returns, generates documentation, and maintains audit trails automatically, transforming compliance from a series of tasks into an uninterrupted operational function that runs silently in the background of the business. Risk management becomes predictive rather than reactive, as

AI models identify emerging exposure before it materializes, simulate alternative actions, and adjust operational parameters dynamically to reduce risk without sacrificing performance, creating a system that actively protects the business rather than simply reporting on past events.

As autonomy increases, the role of humans shifts from execution to governance, oversight, and strategy, where leadership sets risk tolerance, growth objectives, and ethical boundaries, and AI handles the mechanics of compliance within those parameters, ensuring consistency, transparency, and accountability at scale.

In this future state, global compliance is no longer a bottleneck, a cost center, or a source of anxiety, but a foundational capability that enables businesses to operate anywhere, instantly, and confidently, because the rules of every jurisdiction are already understood, applied, and documented automatically, proving that the final evolution of AI in taxation is not assistance, but self-regulation embedded directly into the fabric of global commerce.

"The Company That Never Slept"

When the system went live, there was no ceremony, no countdown, and no dramatic announcement, because the most important transformations rarely announce themselves, they simply begin working, and for Elena, the founder of a borderless digital infrastructure company, that quiet activation marked the moment her business crossed from managing global complexity to transcending it entirely.

In the early years, Elena had built her company with intelligence and caution, expanding methodically into new markets, investing heavily in AI-assisted compliance, and surrounding herself with advisors who understood the risks of cross-border operations, but even with all that preparation, she still felt the constant hum of vigilance, the sense that something somewhere could slip through unnoticed, because as long as humans remained responsible for execution, delay and error were always possible.

The idea of an autonomous tax engine began as a thought experiment during a late-night strategy session, when Elena asked a simple but radical question, what if compliance worked the same way the internet worked, always on, self-correcting, and invisible to the user, and from that moment, the goal shifted from improving compliance to eliminating the need to manage it at all.

The transition took years, integrating systems, training models, validating outcomes, and building governance layers that allowed AI to act independently within defined boundaries, and there were moments of doubt, moments when releasing control felt reckless, but each phase proved itself quietly, filings completed without intervention, taxes calculated perfectly across jurisdictions, documentation assembled instantly when requested, and slowly, the noise of compliance faded into silence.

The first true test came not from the company, but from the world, when a wave of regulatory changes swept through multiple regions simultaneously, overwhelming competitors who scrambled to interpret new rules, delay launches, and halt expansion, while Elena's system absorbed the changes overnight, recalibrated its logic, and continued operating as if nothing had happened, because for the engine, change was not an exception, it was the default state.

As competitors struggled, Elena's company kept moving, entering markets others avoided, pricing products with full after-tax clarity, and reallocating resources dynamically based on real-time regulatory conditions, and what once felt like boldness now felt inevitable, because when compliance is autonomous, hesitation disappears.

Employees noticed the difference before leadership did, because teams no longer waited on approvals, delayed decisions, or feared regulatory missteps, and creativity flourished in an environment where boundaries were enforced automatically and consistently, allowing innovation to accelerate without fear of crossing invisible lines.

Years later, when Elena reflected on the journey, she realized that the most powerful outcome of autonomy was not efficiency or savings, but trust, trust in the system, trust in growth, and trust that the company could operate at global scale without collapsing under its own complexity, and that trust changed how decisions were made at every level.

Standing alone in a quiet office late one evening, watching a live dashboard that showed transactions flowing across continents without interruption, Elena understood that the company no longer slept because it no longer needed to, its intelligence was always awake, always adapting, always compliant, and in that realization, she saw the future of global business, not one where humans race to keep up with complexity, but one where intelligence absorbs complexity entirely, freeing humans to focus on building, imagining, and expanding without fear.

Final Thoughts

The End of Borders in Business Compliance

The journey through this book has revealed a truth that is now unavoidable for modern entrepreneurs, executives, and global operators: borders no longer define where business happens, but they still define where governments claim authority, and the tension between those two realities is where most companies either fail quietly or succeed decisively. Multi-state and international business is no longer an edge case reserved for large corporations; it is the default operating environment for anyone selling online, hiring remotely, licensing intellectual property, or scaling digital products, and yet most businesses still rely on compliance systems designed for a world that no longer exists.

Artificial intelligence is not simply improving tax compliance; it is rewriting the very architecture of how compliance functions inside a business. What once required fragmented teams of accountants, attorneys, payroll specialists, and regional advisors can now be orchestrated through a unified intelligence layer that sees the entire enterprise at once, understands the implications of every transaction, and acts continuously rather than episodically. This shift is not incremental; it is structural, because when intelligence replaces manual interpretation, compliance stops being reactive and becomes intrinsic to how a business operates.

Throughout this book, you have seen how AI maps global tax footprints, automates transactional taxes, manages transfer pricing, mitigates permanent establishment risk, applies tax treaties, prepares audit-ready documentation, adapts to regulatory change, and ultimately transforms compliance into a strategic advantage rather than a burden. These capabilities are not theoretical or futuristic; they are already reshaping how successful businesses operate today, quietly separating those who scale sustainably from those who grow until complexity collapses them.

The most important lesson is not that tax rules are complicated, but that complexity itself is now a competitive filter. Governments are deploying their own AI systems, enforcing rules faster, deeper, and with greater coordination than ever before, and businesses that attempt to keep up using spreadsheets, periodic reviews, or disconnected advisors will increasingly find themselves exposed, not because they acted maliciously, but because they acted slowly. In contrast, companies that embed AI into their compliance infrastructure gain speed, consistency, and foresight, allowing them to operate confidently in environments that intimidate others.

What emerges from this transformation is a new definition of control. Control no longer comes from knowing every rule personally, but from building systems that know the rules better than any individual ever could, apply them instantly, document them perfectly, and evolve alongside them automatically. This is the essence of the autonomous global tax engine: a system that does not wait for instruction, does not forget obligations, and does not panic when conditions change, because change is its native state.

Perhaps the most profound shift is psychological. When compliance becomes automated, transparent, and defensible, fear disappears from decision-making. Expansion stops feeling dangerous. Hiring globally stops feeling risky. New markets stop feeling overwhelming. Instead, growth becomes a calculated, simulated, and guided process, supported by intelligence rather than hope. This is the moment when global business stops being a gamble and becomes an engineered outcome.

As you close this book, understand that the future of business belongs to those who do not treat compliance as an afterthought, a necessary evil, or a sunk cost, but as infrastructure, as critical and foundational as payment systems, data security, or product architecture. AI-driven compliance is not about avoiding penalties; it is about unlocking freedom, freedom to grow, freedom to operate anywhere, and freedom to build without constantly looking over your shoulder.

The companies that thrive in the next decade will not be the ones that move the fastest in isolation, but the ones that move intelligently within a system of rules that grows more complex every year. By embracing AI as the core engine of multi-state and international tax compliance, you are not just preparing for the future, you are aligning your business with it, ensuring that as borders blur and regulations tighten, your company remains resilient, credible, and unstoppable in a truly global economy.

www.ingramcontent.com/pod-product-compliance
Ingram Content Group UK Ltd.
Pitfield, Milton Keynes, MK11 3LW, UK
UKHW020155290926
15471UKWH00005B/890

9 798295 593376